The Ideas of Einstein

The Ideas of

EINSTEIN

DAVID E. FISHER

Illustrated by GWEN BRODKIN

Holt, Rinehart and Winston ☆ New York

Library of Congress Cataloging in Publication Data

Fisher, David E 1932-   The ideas of Einstein.
Summary: Introduces the ideas of Albert Einstein,
focusing on the theory of relativity.
1. Einstein, Albert, 1879-1955—Juvenile literature.
2. Relativity (Physics)—Juvenile literature.
[1. Einstein, Albert, 1879-1955. 2. Relativity
(Physics)]   I.   Title.   QC16.E5F53   530.1'1
80-10423   ISBN 0-03-046516-8

For Sadie,
La Grandmama

Contents

Introduction

☆ Wouldn't it be strange if the laws and rules by which we live were to change without warning? Wouldn't it be strange if policemen suddenly stopped cars for going too *slow* instead of too fast? And if the policeman gave the ticket to *you* instead of to your father? Wouldn't it be strange if one day your mother yelled at you for eating too much broccoli and not enough chocolate cookies?

It would be even stranger if our *scientific* laws and rules changed. If, for example, your friend threw a baseball to you and in midair it changed into a bowling ball! Or if while you were away at school and growing older by a few hours your parents were growing *younger*? You might come home to find yourself older than your father!

That would be a strange world indeed to live in, wouldn't it? But of course such things can't happen.

Or can they?

1

☆

Do You Ever Wonder?

☆ Do you ever wonder?

About what?

About *everything*. Do you ever wonder about the world and the sky and the stars? About why people can't fly and why the sun doesn't fall on our heads? Do you ever wonder about *light*, about where it comes from when you turn on the switch and where it goes when you turn it off?

Most people don't. They have learned that the sun doesn't fall down, and that's enough for them; they don't care about *why*. They know that when they turn on the switch, light will come, and they don't care about where it comes from. They know that when they turn off the switch the light will go away, and they don't care where it goes.

But some people do. Some people care, some people wonder. These are the scientists. They want to understand the world, the universe. They want to know *why* things happen the way they do.

Some scientists wonder mostly about *life*; they are called *biologists*. Others wonder about the *substances* all around us, things like water and air and clothing and automobile tires; these are called *chemists*. Others wonder more about *energy*, about light and gravity and motion; these are called *physicists*.

This book is about the greatest physicist of the twentieth century, some say the greatest of all time. He spent his life wondering and thinking about the simplest question he could think of, but he wasn't satisfied with a simple answer.

His name was Albert Einstein, and the question was:

What is light?

It's a very little question, but no one could tell him the answer. At least, no one could tell him a *good* answer. No one seemed to know, even though light is the most common thing we have around us. It would be very hard to imagine living without light, and yet no one seemed to know what it is, no one could answer his question.

They told him that it was a silly question. They said that light is just light, and what's all the fuss about?

That didn't seem to Einstein to be a good answer. He didn't believe that it was a silly question at all. So he stopped asking about light but he didn't stop thinking about it.

And that was his first discovery: you don't *have* to

believe what people tell you. You can *think* about things as much as you like.

So he kept on thinking about it, and the more he thought about it the more he decided that the problem was that light moves so *fast*. When you turn on the light in the kitchen, it fills the whole room *immediately*. And when you turn it off, it *disappears* immediately.

That must be why we can't see what it really *is*, he thought; it just moves too fast to be seen.

For example, if someone throws a stone at you and it zips right by your head, you can hardly see it because it's moving so fast. When the stone is stopped, when it's lying on the ground, you can see it clearly.

So Einstein thought it must be the same problem with light. If you could *stop* it, then you could see what it really is. But can you stop light? Can you hold it still?

If you're not sure, try an *experiment* (a test to see what will happen). That's what scientists do. Hold a paper bag open and shine some light into it. Then, while the light is still shining, close the bag tight and trap the light in it. Take the bag into a dark room so you can see the light easily, and open the bag and look in. What will you see?

Nothing. The light has disappeared. We *can't* hold it still. But if we can't hold it still, how can we tell what it looks like?

Well, have you ever flown in an airplane? The new jet airliners fly at about 600 miles per hour. That's fast! It's certainly faster than the stone whizzing by your head. But if you are inside the airliner, you can see it as clearly as if it weren't moving at all. That's because you are *moving with it*, moving just as fast.

So Einstein thought that it wouldn't matter that light can't be stopped, if he could only move along with it. If he could do that, he would be able to see it as clearly as a person flying inside an airliner can see the airliner. If he could only do that, what would the light look like?

He never dreamt that this little question about light would lead him to the famous *theory of relativity*, which changed all our laws and rules about things and space and time.

2

☆

The Speed of Light

☆ Einstein was a young boy in school when he first thought of that little question. In fact, he thought about it so much in school that his teachers became angry. Whenever the rest of the class was studying history or singing or learning grammar, Albert was staring out the window, paying no attention to his teacher, daydreaming.

"Albert! What are you doing now?"

"I was looking at the sunlight. I was wondering, what if I could ride along on that sunbeam, go just as fast as it is going—"

"Albert! Such nonsense! You must learn to concentrate on your lessons!"

But he never did. As he grew up, as he passed through his teenage years and into adulthood, he kept thinking about that question.

Other scientists had begun to think about similar questions. They wondered how fast light actually moves. Finally, two American scientists, Albert Mich-

Daydreaming . . .

elson and Edward Morley, did an experiment to actually measure the speed of light.

They bounced a beam of light back and forth between two mirrors and measured how long it took to go the distance between the mirrors. From this they could calculate how fast the light was traveling: its speed. They found that light moves at exactly 186,283 miles per second (or 299,793 kilometers per second). They found that it *always* moves at this speed, even if they themselves were moving along in the same direction as the beam of light or in the opposite direction.

Now, this is very strange. Nothing else moves in this manner. Everything else moves with a speed that de-

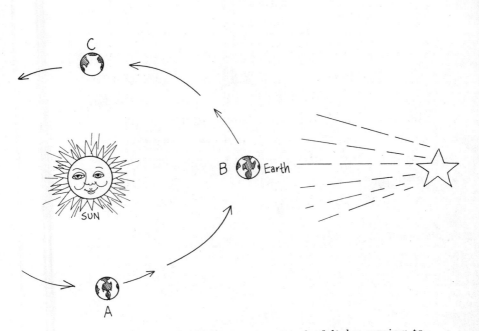

Michelson and Morley measured the speed of light coming to them from the star. They measured it when the earth was traveling toward the star (at point A in its orbit around the sun), when the earth was traveling perpendicular to the light (at point B in its orbit), and when the earth was traveling away from the star (at point C in its orbit). Every time, at points A, B, and C, they found that the speed of light they measured from the star was exactly the same.

pends on the motion of the observer, the person watching. Think of it this way:

Suppose you were standing next to a railroad track and a train came whizzing by. Suppose you knew that the length of a railroad car was exactly 50 feet, and suppose that you wanted to measure how fast it was going, how would you do it?

You would simply measure the time it took for one railroad car to pass you. If it took exactly one-half of a second (that is, one-half second between the time the front of the car passed you and the rear of the car passed you), the train would be moving at a speed of 50 feet every half-second, which is 100 feet every second, right? And if you were *extremely* clever you could figure out that that meant the train had a speed of 68 miles per hour.

Because 100 feet per second is 6,000 feet per minute.

$$100 \times 60 = 6,000$$

And 6,000 feet per minute is 360,000 feet per hour.

$$6,000 \times 60 = 360,000$$

And since there are 5,280 feet in a mile, 360,000 feet per hour is 68 miles per hour.

$$360,000 \div 5,280 = 360,000/5,280 = 68$$

Now, just to make sure you understand all that, figure out how fast the train would be going if it took one second for the railroad car to pass you. (Answer: 34 miles per hour.)

Now suppose you were to do the same experiment while driving along in a car on a road next to the railroad track. Suppose someone was driving the car at 34 miles per hour. If you were going in the same direction

Watching the train go by.

One-half second later.

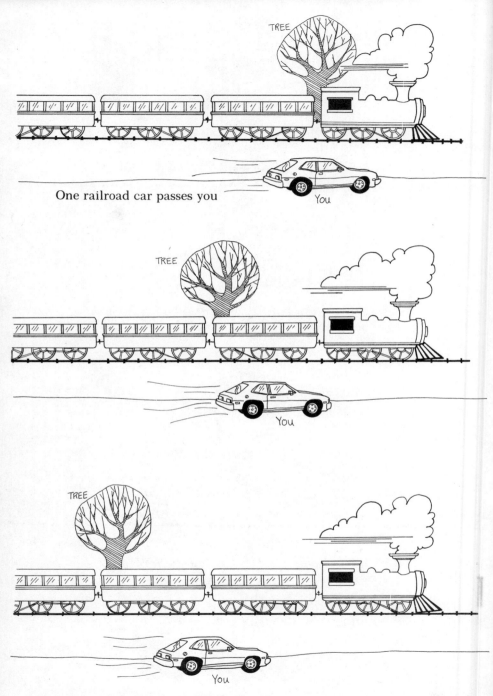

One railroad car passes you

while two pass the tree in one whole second.

as the train, which is going at 68 miles per hour, how long would it take for each railroad car to pass you?

If you think about it (or if you get someone to take you for a ride and try it), you will see that it takes each car twice as long to pass you; it will take one second instead of one-half second. So you must say that *compared to you* the train is only going 34 miles per hour, although compared to the street or the railroad tracks it is still going 68 miles per hour.

But what is the *real* speed of the railroad train? You might be tempted to say that the real speed is 68 miles per hour, but if you are, try to resist that temptation. Because you would be wrong.

What if there were a man on Mars looking at the train through a telescope? He would agree that it was going 34 miles per hour relative to you in your car or 68 miles per hour relative to the earth, but he can see that the earth itself is zooming around the sun at a speed of 67,000 miles per hour. So, relative to the sun, the train is zipping along at 67,068 miles per hour (if it is moving in the same direction as the earth). And compared to himself on Mars, which is itself speeding around the sun at 54,000 miles per hour, the train would be moving at a speed of—well, you see it gets very complicated. And even if you went ahead and figured that out, what if the train were also being observed by somebody standing on Venus? Or Saturn? Or in a spaceship?

You are sitting there on earth measuring the motion of the train. But the observers on Mars, Venus, and the spaceship can see that you are not sitting still but are moving as the earth moves around the sun. And each of these observers is moving in a different direction, so your motion is different to each of them. So what is your "real" motion? Since everybody gives a different answer to this question, we have to say that there *is* no answer: there is no such thing as "real" motion.

All of these people would measure different speeds for the train *relative to themselves*. How could they agree on which is the *real* speed?

So Einstein said there is no such thing as a real speed: all motion is relative. By this he meant that the speed of anything is relative to the person making the measurement. Different people who measure the speed of the train—the person standing near the track, the person in the car, etc.—will get different speeds, and none is the "real" speed.

Now Einstein came back to the question of light. What would happen if you did the same kind of experiment with a beam of light? Suppose you go with your friend Bill to an empty field in the middle of the night. You each have a watch, and each watch is set to exactly the same time. Then you leave Bill there in the middle of the field and you measure off a certain distance; let's say you measured off exactly 186,283 miles (or 299,793 kilometers) from him. Then, at exactly midnight, you shine a flashlight at him. If the speed of light is really constant with a value of 186,283 miles per second, as Michelson and Morley claimed, your friend would see the flash of light exactly one second later, at one second past midnight.

But suppose Bill has a twin sister. You left him standing out in the middle of the field at midnight. And his twin sister, Sandy, owns a rocket ship! And suppose that Sandy's rocket ship could whiz along at a speed of 186,283 miles per second.

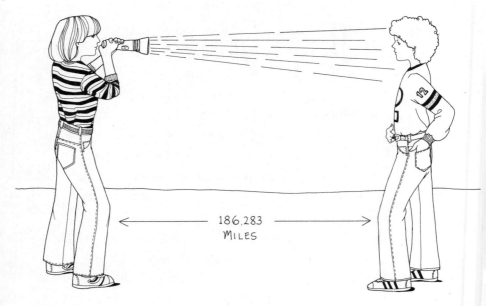

186,283
MILES

Now let's do the experiment again, but this time, when you shine your flashlight at Bill, Sandy will zoom off in her rocketship from you to him. How long will it take her to go from you to Bill?

If she is traveling 186,283 miles per second, that means that in one second she will travel 186,283 miles, right? And since Bill is standing 186,283 miles away, it will take her exactly one second to get there.

Now, what if Sandy had also measured the speed of the light beam from your flashlight? Wouldn't she find that relative to herself it hadn't moved at all? (Since both she and the beam of light started together at you and finished together at Bill.)

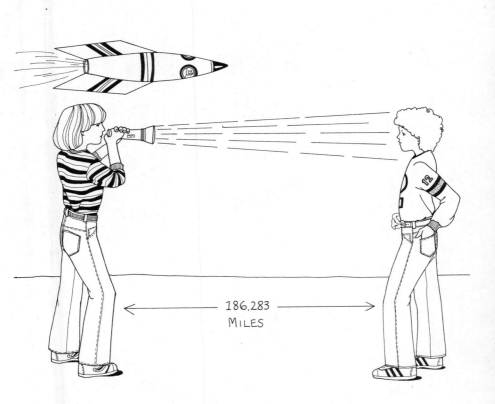

186,283
MILES

But that would mean that relative to her the speed of light was zero. And Michelson and Morley had just proved that the speed of light is always the same for everybody! So what *would* happen if Sandy measured the speed of the beam of light?

Einstein couldn't actually do the experiment, and neither could anyone else, because nobody really has a rocket ship that can go 186,283 miles per second. Our fastest jets and rockets can't go anywhere near that fast. But Einstein could *think* about it, couldn't he? He

If a rocketship was moving at 186,283 miles per second, would it really be going as fast as light? Is that possible? Einstein wondered.

could think about what would happen if we really had a rocket ship that could go as fast as light.

And so he sat there and thought about it. He thought about it and he wondered about it, and so did the world's greatest physicists in every country on earth. None of them could figure out what would happen, until finally Einstein suggested that perhaps there is no solution to this problem. Perhaps they should stop worrying about it and instead start all over in their thinking about the laws of motion.

But where should they start? Well, what did they actually *know*? They knew that ordinary motion, like the speed of an automobile or a jet or a train, is relative to whomever is observing it. They also knew that the Michelson-Morley experiment showed that the speed of light is *not* relative, but is *absolute*: it is always 186,283 miles per second. Perhaps we should just accept those two statements as basic truths, and go on from there.

And that is what Einstein did. He said that there are two rules for motion. Rule # 1: All motion is relative. Rule # 2: *Except* the speed of light, which is absolute and always constant.

How did this explain anything? If Einstein were right, then the beam of light from your flashlight would still reach Bill at exactly one second past midnight, and so would Sandy in her rocket ship. But now Sandy in her rocket ship would say that *relative to her*

likewise also

the light was still moving at the same speed! And if the light was moving ahead faster than she was, then certainly it would have to reach Bill before she did!

But Bill would say: "No, the light and Sandy both reached me at the same time."

Who would be right? Would the light reach Bill at the same time or before her? It couldn't do *both*!

Or could it?

Actually, Einstein said that this question has no "real" answer—that the question of when the light reaches Bill has *different* answers. Sandy's answer is that the light reaches Bill first, and Bill's answer is that both the light and Sandy reach him at the same time—and they're both right!

How can that be? Because, Einstein explained, the very nature of space and time are changed when Sandy—or anyone else—travels at speeds near the speed of light. Space and time are not "real," as we always thought, but instead they are *relative* to different people moving at different speeds.

But then what *is* "real"? Is *anything* real? As the poet Edgar Allan Poe asked,

> Is *all* that we see or seem
> but a dream within a dream?

When Einstein finally found the answer to that question, he changed our whole world.

3

The Theory of Relativity

☆ Einstein thought and thought about this problem for a long time. If the speed of light was 186,283 miles per second for everyone, then Sandy and the beam of light could not arrive at Bill at the same time: because that would mean that *relative to Sandy* the beam of light hadn't moved. But *relative to Bill* both Sandy and the beam of light were moving with the same speed, so they'd *have* to get there at the same time! This was certainly a puzzle.

Finally Einstein was forced to accept the conclusion that if the world around us really behaved the way we thought it did, his two rules were impossible. The speed of light could *not* be constant for everybody. But Michelson and Morley had proven that it was!

Slowly he began to wonder if perhaps the world is *not* the way we think it is. Perhaps all the rules of space and time and speed should be changed. Perhaps he could discover a whole new set of laws or rules which would allow his two rules to be possible. This was an exciting thought!

At this time he was a clerk in the patent office in Berne, a lovely little town in Switzerland. Every day, when he had finished the work he was paid to do, he would sit and think about this problem.

Finally, after years of struggling, he came upon the solution. And once he did, our world was never the same again.

How did he solve the problem? By using mathematics. He realized that mathematics may be hard to learn, but once you learn it it's really useful for solving problems. Because it always gives you the right answer. Always.

For example, once you learn that one plus one is two, you know that one anything plus one anything is *always* two anythings. If someone asks you how many apples are one apple plus one apple, you don't have to ask if the apples are red or green or fresh or rotten. You know the answer: two apples.

So Einstein decided he would use mathematics to try to answer his tough problem. In his spare time after work he studied more and more mathematics, and finally, after years of struggling, he came upon the solution.

He called his solution the *theory of relativity*. He called it that because he found that, except for the constant speed of light, all other motion is relative to whomever is measuring it. Except for light, there is no such thing as *real* motion.

Then he said that time and space are relative too!

But what does that mean?

It means that in the experiment, when you and Bill were standing in the field in the middle of the night, you both agreed that it took the beam of light from your flashlight one second to travel the measured distance. But according to Einstein's theory, Sandy, in her rocket ship, would agree with nothing except that the speed of light was constant! She would say that it took much less than one second for her trip, and that the distance was much less than 186,283 miles. That is because her space and time are different from yours! And if you checked her watch, you would find that it no longer agreed with yours, even though you had set them together just before the experiment. And as she zipped past you, you would say that her whole rocket ship looked shorter than it did when it was sitting on the ground!

Hey, what's going on?!

What's going on, Einstein explained, is that time and space behaved differently for Sandy because she was in motion. The behavior of time and space is not *real* (he used the word *absolute*) but *relative*.

What does that mean? Well, you already know that some things are *relative*. Wind, for example: if you are standing still on a calm day you feel no wind, but if you run down the street you will feel a breeze on your face. The question of whether or not there is a wind depends on whether you are standing still or are in motion: there is *no absolute* answer to that question. The answer is relative. And don't forget, the faster you are in motion, the greater the wind.

Other things are *absolute*, like rain: it doesn't matter whether you are standing still outside or running around. If it's raining you are going to get wet. The question of whether or not it's raining does not depend on your motion. It is not *relative*.

Einstein's mathematics now told us that time and space, which we had always believed were *absolute* (like the rain), were in fact *relative* (like the wind): their effect on us depends on whether or not we are in motion, and how fast we are going. For example, since time is relative, people don't get older at the same rate. Sandy in the rocket ship—or any person in motion— would not get older as fast as you and Bill standing still on the ground!

4

---☆

Time Dilatation

☆ This result of relativity—that time is not real but is relative—is called *time dilatation*: it says that time flows more slowly for a person in motion, so that all his clocks and calendars run slow, and therefore he will get older more slowly.

Let's take the twins Bill and Sandy again. Bill stays on earth while Sandy goes off in her rocket ship to the stars. If the rocket ship travels at 99.99 percent the speed of light, and if the rocket trip to the stars and back takes fifty years, do you know what will happen when Sandy comes home? Bill will be fifty years older, of course. But Sandy will still be a little kid! She'll only be half a year older than when she started!

In fact, Einstein said her clocks on the rocket ship (and her calendar) will have told her that the trip took only six months. Unless she knows all about Einstein's theory of relativity, she would be shocked that her twin brother Bill—and *everyone* on earth—is so much older.

Sounds silly, doesn't it? If your father were forty

Sandy and Bill—twins!

years old and you were ten, and if he went on such a trip, when he came back he would still be forty years old but you would be sixty! You'd be older than your own father!

But is it really so silly, Einstein asked? It *sounds* silly, but do we *know* that it is silly? The only way to know for sure is to do the experiment—fly off in a rocket ship—and see what happens. The problem is that the rocket ship has to go at nearly the speed of light, and we can't make anything that will fly that fast.

Einstein suggested time dilatation in 1905. It was not possible to test it by experiment then. But nearly seventy years later, in 1971, scientists had learned to make atomic clocks that could measure time accurately to a few billionths of a second, and with such accurate clocks they were able to test Einstein's idea. One of the clocks they set on the ground, at the U.S. Naval Observatory, and the other they flew around the world on a jet airliner at a speed of about 600 miles per hour. Now 600 miles per hour is nowhere near as fast as the speed of light, but it's fast enough that—if Einstein were correct—they should see a very small effect. If Einstein was right, when the two clocks came back together again at the Naval Observatory (after one of them had flown around the world) they would no longer show the same time. Their times should be different by a few billionths of a second.

And when the scientists looked, the clocks *were* different. By a few billionths of a second!

They could calculate that this change meant that, if the clock had been traveling at a speed 99.99 percent the speed of light, when fifty years had gone by on earth only a half year would have gone by for the traveling clock.

Einstein's theory of relativity was correct!

5

☆

Mass

☆ Einstein's theory said even stranger things. It said that if an object were in motion, not only would its time slow down but its mass would increase. The *mass* of an object is the amount of stuff in it. What we usually call its weight. The theory of relativity says that if something is moving, it gets heavier!

If, for example, Bill throws you a baseball, as it moves through the air it actually gets heavier. If it's moving fast enough, by the time it gets to you it will weigh as much as a bowling ball!

But Einstein can't kid you. You know that this doesn't happen. You've *done* this experiment, right? You've thrown baseballs back and forth, and they didn't become bowling balls, right?

Wrong. Because you didn't throw them *fast* enough. Einstein's theory says the balls have to go at nearly the speed of light for the increase in mass to be noticeable. Next time you go to a baseball game, take a watch and see how long it takes a pitcher to throw the ball across the plate. The *fastest* fastball in the major leagues takes about half a second to reach the plate. That means its speed is 90 feet per half-second or 180 feet per second; that's about 125 miles per hour, or much less than one mile per second. That's *nowhere* near the speed of light. If you could throw a baseball at 99 percent the speed of light, not only could no one hit it, but you'd kill the catcher! It would weigh as much as a bowling ball!

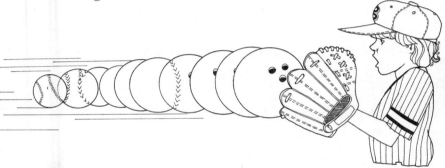

A baseball thrown at 99% the speed of light would weigh as much as a bowling ball.

But how do we know this is true? Because, again, an experiment has been made.

In 1896, shortly before Einstein worked out his theory, a French scientist named Antoine Henri Becquerel discovered a strange *natural phenomenon*. He discovered that an ordinary-looking white powder called uranium oxide was giving off energy. Other scientists (particularly Marie Curie in France and Ernest Rutherford in Canada) studied this strange phenomenon and found that the uranium *atoms* were breaking apart and throwing out not only energy but also tiny particles smaller than atoms! This was called *radioactivity*. Some of the particles, called *electrons*, were being shot out at nearly the speed of light. So when the theory of relativity predicted that a moving object's mass should increase, scientists set out to measure the speed and the mass of the electrons very carefully.

And they found, to their amazement, that the electrons whizzing out at nearly the speed of light weighed more than the same electrons when they weren't moving! And they weighed *exactly* as much more as the theory of relativity had predicted.

Victory number two for Albert!

6

Boom!

☆ While he was working out his theory, Einstein discovered a new equation which at first he didn't understand. The equation was:

$$E = mc^2$$

In this equation E stands for energy and m for mass; c is the speed of light and c^2 is the speed of light squared, or multiplied times itself. The equation didn't seem to make much sense, because energy and mass are so different from each other. Energy is often measured as heat, and mass as weight; things that are hotter have more energy, and things that are heavier have more mass. The equation seemed to say that any object with a certain mass, such as a stone, also had energy. But what energy does a stone have? Can a stone give off heat?

In fact, the equation says that the stone has an *awful lot* of energy, because the amount of energy (E) is mc^2, which is the mass of the stone times the awfully big number, c^2. That much energy would give enough heat to make a *fire*; in fact a *big* fire; in fact an *explosion*; in fact, the *biggest* explosion the world has ever seen!

But the rock doesn't explode, does it? It just sits there quietly minding its own business, ignoring you and me and Einstein.

You will remember from the last chapter that near the time Einstein discovered the theory of relativity, in 1905, there was a great mystery in the world. The French scientist Henri Becquerel had discovered that uranium was radioactive, remember? And this meant that the atoms of uranium continually gave off energy. A few years later, Madame Curie had discovered a new kind of atom that was even more radioactive: radium. The atoms of radium gave off so much energy that a bottle filled with radium would stay warm forever, even if it were kept in a refrigerator. And nobody knew where the radium's heat—its energy—came from.

Einstein suggested that it came from $E = mc^2$. He suggested that when an atom was radioactive some of its mass disappeared, and this mass was changed into energy. So the result of the radioactivity would be *smaller* atoms, but *warm* ones.

And when scientists measured the masses of the radioactive atoms, they found that he was right.

Victory number three for Albert!

Many years later, in the 1940s, scientists learned how to control this *atomic energy*. When they did, they took a few pounds of the proper material and created a fire; in fact a *big* fire; in fact an *explosion*; in fact, the *biggest* explosion the world had ever seen! They learned how to do it in the nick of time. America was then in the midst of a terrible war, the Second World War. By 1945, America and England had defeated Germany and were clearly winning against their other antagonist, Japan. But Japan refused to surrender. In the summer of that year the Allied forces were planning to invade Japan, and Japan was preparing to defend herself dearly against the onslaught. Our generals estimated that between one and two *million* lives would be lost!

And then, that summer, a group of scientists finally managed to unleash the atomic energy. They built two atomic bombs and with each of them destroyed a whole city, and Japan saw that further struggle was useless. The surrender saved more than a million American, British, and Japanese lives that would have been lost in the invasion.

The atomic bomb—a terrible thing, surely—had ended the worst war the world had ever seen. So thank God—or Einstein—for that.

7

Gravity

☆ The successes of Einstein's theory of relativity made him the most famous person in the world, and his equation $E = mc^2$ was known to everybody from schoolboys to kings (even though most of them, schoolboys *and* kings, didn't understand what it meant).

Still, he was not satisfied. You see, in his theory he had ignored *gravity*, even though he knew that gravity is the most important force in the universe. He had ignored it on purpose, because it made his equations too complicated. But now he wanted to try again, to understand how gravity would fit into his new theory of relativity.

But what is gravity? Up until the twentieth century, everything we knew about gravity had been described by the man who discovered its existence, the English scientist Isaac Newton, who lived in the seventeenth century. When people argue about who was the greatest scientist of all time, the two finalists are almost always Einstein and Newton.

Schoolboys and kings confused by $E = mc^2$.

Newton had showed that the moon moves around the earth and the earth moves around the sun because of the force of gravity. It's also gravity that keeps us from flying off the surface of the earth, and makes apples fall off the trees.

This is because gravity is a *universal attractive* force. *Universal* means that it exists everywhere in the universe, between all objects: the sun attracts the earth, the earth attracts the moon, the moon attracts the tides. *Attractive* means that gravity pulls the objects toward each other. They are *attracted* to each other according to their masses: the greater the mass, the greater the force of gravity.

But where does this force of gravity come from? What causes it? Newton *described* gravity, but he never *explained* it. He simply said that it exists. And for more than two hundred years that satisfied everyone.

It didn't satisfy Einstein. He wanted to understand what gravity really is. He saw that his theory of relativity had given a new explanation of time and space and mass, and now he wondered if it could explain gravity as well.

So he got back to work. He soon realized that all his equations became much more complicated when gravity was included, and that he would have to learn a whole new kind of mathematics to solve this problem. This new kind of mathematics, called *tensors*, was able to describe such things as curved space and curved time, but was even more complicated than the algebra and calculus he had used in his theory of relativity. He thought of that theory now as a *special* theory of relativity, because it was useful only for the special case where gravity was unimportant.

It took him more than ten years, but finally he had solved the *general* theory of relativity, in which gravity was included. And when he had, he had penetrated the innermost secrets of the universe.

We had always thought about the universe in terms of *space* and *time*. But Einstein now saw that this way of thinking was not quite right. Instead, space and time must be considered together, and when they are, gravity turns out to be simply a *curvature* in the *space-time* of our universe.

If space-time is curved, this means that anything moving in our universe must follow a curved path, and this is what happens under the force of gravity. You don't understand? Well, try to jump up. What happens? You jumped up, and it was the force in your legs that moved you up. But you also came down again, didn't you? The force in your legs moved you up, and the force of gravity brought you back down again. If you were to draw a picture of the path you followed in your jump, it would be a curve.

In much the same way, the earth and the sun and the moon all curve around one another, and none of

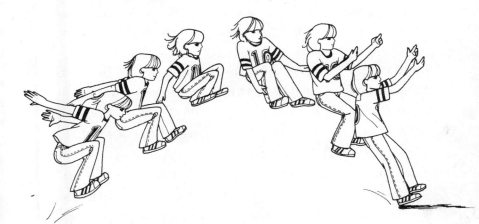

The curved path of a jumping person (gravitational pull).

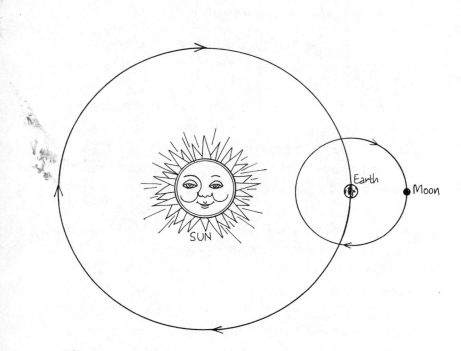

The moon is circling around the earth at the same time that the earth is circling around the sun. They move in these curved paths around each other because of the curvature of space-time.

them ever fall down. They move in this way because space-time is curved, and this curvature is what gravity really is.

Well, all this was a completely new idea of gravity, quite different from Newton's description of it. When Einstein explained his new general theory, people naturally wondered if it were true. Again, as with the special theory, they wanted experimental proof.

And again, as with the special theory, they got it.

8

☆

The Mysterious Motion
of Mercury

☆ Astronomers (scientists who study the stars and planets) had known for a long time that something was wrong with Mercury.

Mercury is the planet closest to the sun. Its path around the sun (its *orbit*) is nearly a perfect ellipse, as Newton's explanation of gravity had said it should be. An ellipse is a squashed-down circle, and if you run your finger around the edge of it, each time your finger goes around the whole ellipse it comes back to the same point.

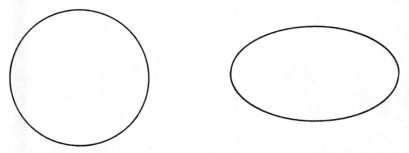

But Mercury's orbit is not quite a perfect ellipse, and each time Mercury completes its passage around its orbit, it doesn't come back *quite* to the same point. The same is true for *all* the planets, but because Mercury is the closest planet to the sun—where the sun's gravity is strongest—it is the only one where this is noticeable.

The problem of *why* Mercury doesn't come back to the same point had puzzled astronomers ever since Mercury was discovered in 1845. Because, you see, Newton's theory of gravity predicted that it should come back to *exactly* the same spot each time around. The only thing that could cause it not to, they thought, was if there were another, unknown planet next to the sun. So they searched and searched with their telescopes for this planet, but they could not discover it.

Einstein wondered if his new general theory of relativity would also predict that Mercury should come back to the same spot each time. So he solved his equations, and found that in this theory Mercury would *not* be expected to come back perfectly each time. In fact, his theory said that Mercury should behave in *exactly* the manner it was observed to behave.

Well, that was all very fine, but in order to be convinced that he was right, Einstein wanted his theory to tell him something new, something that had never been observed before.

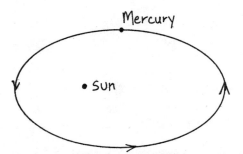

If Mercury's ellipse was perfect, it would look like this. Mercury would follow the same path forever.

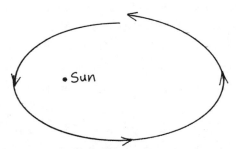

But it is not perfect; Mercury does not come back to the same point.

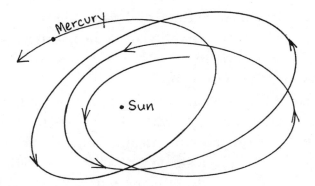

And so its path looks like this.

9

The Bending of Starlight

☆ Einstein now tried to combine the subject that had first interested him, light, with his new general theory of relativity. According to Newton's theory, gravity is an attractive force that exists between every object in the universe. But an object is something you can pick up, touch, feel. Light is not an object: you can see it, but you cannot pick it up or touch it or feel it. Since it is not an object, according to Newton, light should not be affected by gravity.

But Einstein's general theory told him that gravity was a curve in space-time, and *anything* traveling in curved space-time would have to curve: light *would* be affected by gravity.

Here was something new indeed! But how could it be tested? For Einstein was able to figure out that the effect of gravity on light would be very slight: remember that experiment with Bill and Sandy in the field at midnight? When you shone your flashlight at Bill, the beam of light would not come out of the flashlight, bend over, and fall to the ground! It would keep going straight. That is because the gravity of the whole earth is not enough to bend a beam of light.

But the gravity of the sun is much stronger than that of the earth. Einstein was able to calculate that the curvature of space-time around the sun (its gravity) would be enough to bend a beam of light. But how did that help? He couldn't go stand on the sun and shine a flashlight to see if the light bends, could he? For one thing, there's no air conditioning up there, so it would be uncomfortably warm. (Can you think of four more reasons?)

Never mind, Einstein said, we can use a beam of starlight. When a beam of starlight passes close by the sun, it should be bent enough for us to see it.

But the sun is so much brighter than the starlight that we would never be able to see the starlight at all when the sun is out!

Then, Einstein said, we shall have to wait for an *eclipse* of the sun.

An eclipse of the sun occurs when the moon passes between the sun and the earth. Then the earth is in the shadow of the moon and the sunlight is blotted out, and starlight can be seen just as if it were nighttime.

So, Einstein said, let us wait for the next eclipse and then observe the light of the stars very carefully with our best telescopes. If the general theory of relativity is correct, the starlight which passes quite close to the sun should be observed to bend.

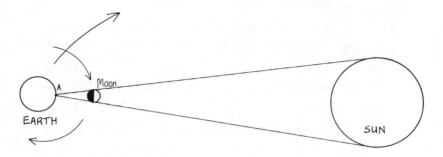

Eclipse of the sun occurs at point A on earth. When the moon moves between the sun and earth, it blocks out the sunlight at point A. The rest of the earth can still see the sun normally.

Eclipses occur on earth about twice every three years, but they occur only at specific locations on the surface of the earth. Since most of the surface of the earth is covered with oceans or inaccessible jungles or mountains or snow or desert, it is very seldom that an eclipse takes place where it is possible to see it.

The next eclipse was to occur in 1919 in Africa and South America, just three years after Einstein made his calculations. And when the eclipse came, there were scientists waiting by their telescopes to look up at the starlight to see if it would indeed bend as it came around the sun.

And indeed it did bend, just as Einstein had predicted!

10

☆

From Here to Eternity

☆ Einstein's general theory of relativity was hailed by scientists all over the world as "the greatest achievement in the history of human thought." With it we can probe the mysteries of the universe, unlocking the secrets of the smallest atoms and the largest stars, and even peer into the moment of creation itself. We can carry out scientific research that is important for everyone on earth, enabling us to solve our energy problems; and we can carry out scientific research that is pure fun.

Example # 1: The mysteries of the universe. People had always thought of the universe as *static*. This means unchanging, eternal. But when Einstein solved his equations for the whole universe, he found that the solutions are what scientists call *time-dependent*. This means that the solutions will be different at different times, and it must also mean that the universe itself is different at different times.

This tells us that the universe must have had a definite beginning, and even now is changing. Shortly after Einstein discovered this, astronomers found proof that the stars in distant galaxies are rushing away from us!

Since they are rushing away from us (and from one another), we say that the universe is expanding, growing bigger day by day and year by year. This is a far from a static universe! We can calculate that in y long past the universe was much smaller, and that the stars were much closer together. If we conti the calculation, we find that there must have be time when all the stars and planets were squ together into one enormous ball. Then, with mendous bang, this enormous ball exploded a everything hurtling out into space.

And just a few years ago, in the 1970s, we h able to detect evidence of that ancient which created our universe. It is called the and Einstein's theory was the first hint we was in such a Bang that our universe was

Example #2: Nuclear energy. About years ago, when it got dark out, people w Our civilization has been freeing itself mor from the limits and dangers of the natu When it gets dark out now, we simply t lights. When it gets cold we turn on the when it gets hot we turn on the air conditi want to go somewhere too far to walk we g or even fly through the air. If ancient peo us today, they would think we were gods!

But all of this takes energy. We get our energy from burning trees or coal or oil or gas. And we are burning too much. We need too much energy for our cars and air conditioners and factories and television. It takes many years to grow a tree, and *millions* of years to form oil and coal and gas.

We *need* the energy, yet we are running out of fuel. So what will we do? There are two things we can do. First, we can all conserve energy. We can walk to the store instead of riding, and put on a sweater instead of turning on the heat. And second, we can use Einstein's equation $E = mc^2$ to generate nuclear energy from uranium.

There are many problems with nuclear energy, but scientists are working hard to solve them. If they succeed, we will have enough energy to get us through the crisis period of the next fifty years. If they don't, get prepared to do a lot of walking with lots of sweaters.

Example #3: Black holes. This is probably the most fascinating and fun topic in science today. It began when an Indian scientist named Chandrasekhar said that if the sun can bend light—as Einstein showed—it might be possible for a supergiant star to bend light so much that it would bend right around in a circle and fall back into the star! In this case no light would ever escape from the star. The star could not be seen. It would be a black hole in space.

Today some scientists think that there may be such

You can see a normal star because its rays of light reach your eyes. But the light from a black hole is bent by the enormous gravity and falls back into the black hole. So the light rays never reach your eyes and you can't see it.

black holes in the center of distant galaxies, and that entire stars may be falling into them and disappearing! Inside such black holes, space-time may be very different from what it is to us, and so these ideas are very exciting. Nobody knows if anything useful will come out of looking for black holes or thinking about them, but who knows? When Einstein first began wondering about light, he never thought that anything as wonderful and useful as the theory of relativity would come out of it.

He never thought that the nature of light would have anything to do with understanding gravity, for example, or finding the secret of nuclear energy—the secret that may save our civilization from energy starvation. That is what is so much fun about science: you never know where the search may take you. Out into space to the stars and black holes, or down into the tiny atom; back in time to the creation of the universe, or forward in time to the end of the world.

The search continues. Who knows where else it may take us?

Definitions

Absolute: constant, not dependent upon varying conditions.

Atom: one of the tiny, invisible particles which make up the universe. Atoms are made up of three parts: electrons, neutrons, and protons (see below).

Big Bang: the theory which says that our universe was created in one gigantic explosion. Scientists arrived at this theory with the help of Einstein's discoveries.

Black hole: a very dense star which traps light in its field of gravity instead of giving it off, and cannot be seen as a result.

Curvature: the curved path that gravity forces all things to follow.

Eclipse: occurs when the moon passes between the sun and the earth. The moon blots out sunlight to the earth and makes for a darkness just like nighttime.

Electron, neutron, and proton: the three parts of an atom. *Neutrons* and *protons* fit together in the *nucleus* or center of the atom while the electrons move around them outside of the nucleus.

Energy: the ability to move things, or do work. Energy can be in different forms: light, heat, electricity, etc.

Experiment: what scientists perform to see what will happen, when they are trying to find something out about the natural world.

Gravity: the natural force which controls the movement of all bodies. It keeps all the planets moving in their proper positions around the sun and keeps humans from flying off the earth's surface. It is a *universal attractive* force: it exists everywhere in the universe and works by pulling objects towards each other.

Mass: the amount of matter in an object, that makes it heavy or light.

Natural phenomenon: something that occurs in nature which can be sensed (heard or seen or felt or smelled or tasted).

Nuclear energy: the energy which holds the nuclei of atoms together; it can be released in radioactivity.

Orbit: the path around one object which another object follows, such as the path around the sun which each planet follows.

Radioactivity: the process by which atoms break up and throw out energy and particles. They become smaller and different atoms.

Relative: not absolute (see above), but dependent upon something else. For example, the speed of an object depends on the speed of the person measuring it.

Space-time: Einstein said that space and time are not separate, but must be considered together. We live in the United States in the twentieth century—that is our space-time.

Theory of relativity: Einstein's famous theory which says that light always moves at the same speed, but the speed of anything else that moves depends upon who or what is measuring it.

Time-dilatation: results from relativity and means that time flows more slowly for someone in motion, so that he or she will get older more slowly.

Index

About the Author

Dr. DAVID E. FISHER, cosmochemist and physicist at the University of Miami, is the author of *The Creation of Atoms and Stars* and *Creation of the Universe*. He also writes novels.

About the Artist

GWEN BRODKIN, a free-lance illustrator and native New Yorker, has illustrated *The Herb & Spice Book for Kids* and *It Will Never Be the Same Again*.